SOVEREIGN LORD

A MUSICAL PROCLAIMING THE RISEN, CONQUERING KING

CREATED *by* PHIL MEHRENS

ARRANGED AND ORCHESTRATED *by* DAVE WILLIAMSON

ALLEGIS
PUBLICATIONS

Copyright © 2008 by Pilot Point Music,
Box 419527, Kansas City, MO 64141.
All rights reserved. Litho in U.S.A.

AllegisPublications.com

Contents

Praise to the Lord, the Almighty 5

Praise to the Lord, the Almighty – Underscore 18

He Will Rule the World *with* Hosanna, Loud Hosanna 20

He Will Rule the World – Underscore 34

To Save 35

Most High – Underscore 45

Son of the Most High 46

Narration 54

Sovereign Lord 55

Narration 68

What a Great Morning 69

Narration 80

Enthroned 81

Enthroned – Underscore 89

Revelation Song 90

Sovereign Lord Finale 100

    Includes: Praise to the Lord, the Almighty – He Will Rule the World

Praise to the Lord, the Almighty

Copyright © 2008 by Pilot Point Music (ASCAP). All rights reserved.
Administered by The Copyright Company, PO Box 128139, Nashville, TN 37212-8139.

PLEASE NOTE: Copying of this product is NOT covered by CCLI licenses. For CCLI information call 1-800-234-2446.

Praise to the Lord, the Almighty
Underscore

Stralsund Gesangbuch
Arr. by Dave Williamson

*ALL: Who believed what we have heard? To whom has the arm of the Lord been revealed? "Behold, the days are coming, says the LORD, when I will raise up for David a righteous Branch, and he shall reign as king and deal wisely." (Jer 23:5)

LADIES: Rejoice greatly, O Daughter of Zion! Shout, Daughter of Jerusalem! See, your king comes to you, righteous and having salvation, gentle and riding on a donkey . . . (Zec 9:9)

MEN: . . . Jerusalem shall be called the throne of the LORD, and all nations shall gather to it, to the presence of the LORD in Jerusalem . . . (Jer 3:17)

ALL: ". . . I am coming to gather all nations and tongues; and they shall come and shall see my glory . . . (Isa 66:18) And the glory of the LORD shall be revealed, and all flesh shall see it together, for the mouth of the LORD has spoken." (Isa 40:5)

MEN: Pass through, pass through the gates! Prepare the way for the people. Build up, build up the highway! Remove the stones. Raise a banner for the nations.

LADIES: The LORD has made proclamation to the ends of the earth: "Say to the Daughter of Zion, 'See, your Saviour comes! *(He Will Rule the World begins)* See, his reward is with him . . .'" *(Isa 62:10-11)*

ALL: Prepare the way of the Lord! Hosanna to the Son of David, the King of all the earth!

Arr. © 2008 by Pilot Point Music (ASCAP). All rights reserved.
Administered by The Copyright Company, PO Box 128139, Nashville, TN 37212-8139.

PLEASE NOTE: Copying of this product is NOT covered by CCLI licenses. For CCLI information call 1-800-234-2446.

He Will Rule the World

with
Hosanna, Loud Hosanna

Words and Music by
PHIL MEHRENS
Arr. by Dave Williamson

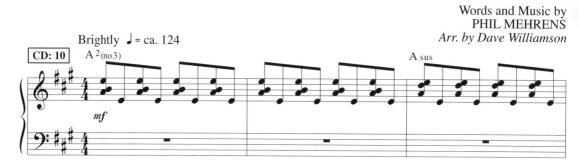

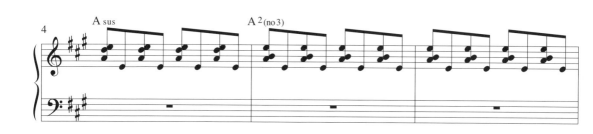

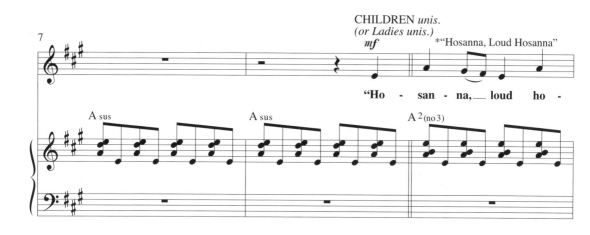

---

*Words by JEANNETTE THRELFALL; Music *Gesangbuch der herzogl.* Arr. © 2008 by Pilot Point Music (ASCAP). All rights reserved.
Administered by The Copyright Company, PO Box 128139, Nashville, TN 37212-8139.

Copyright © 2008 by Pilot Point Music (ASCAP). All rights reserved.
Administered by The Copyright Company, PO Box 128139, Nashville, TN 37212-8139.

PLEASE NOTE: Copying of this product is NOT covered by CCLI licenses. For CCLI information call 1-800-234-2446.

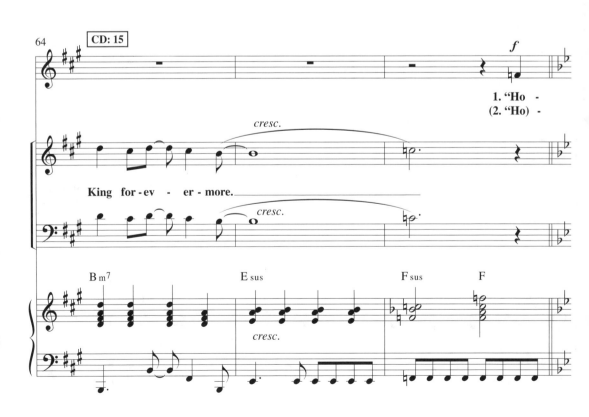

He Will Rule the World

Underscore

PHIL MEHRENS
Arr. by Dave Williamson

NARRATOR *(without music)*: When Jesus entered Jerusalem on the day we call "Palm Sunday," there were great crowds because of His powerful miracles, *(music begins)* because of His astounding teachings and especially because He had raised His friend Lazarus from the dead.

They had so many expectations about Him. They knew so many scriptures that had to be fulfilled in Him. Before Jesus came, John the Baptizer had preached powerfully in the desert, bringing the whole nation of Israel to repentance with the explosive promise that "the kingdom of heaven is at hand." *(To Save begins)* The destined time had arrived to "prepare the way of the Lord." Their Messiah, the true king of Israel was on His way.

But the people's excitement was mixed with uncertainty. If our King, the Son of the Most High comes, What will He be like? What will He do? What will He expect of us?

Copyright © 2008 by Pilot Point Music (ASCAP). All rights reserved.
Administered by The Copyright Company, PO Box 128139, Nashville, TN 37212-8139.

PLEASE NOTE: Copying of this product is NOT covered by CCLI licenses. For CCLI information call 1-800-234-2446.

To Save

Words and Music by
PHIL MEHRENS, STEVE MARSHALL
and DONNA JAREE BROOKS
Arr. by Dave Williamson

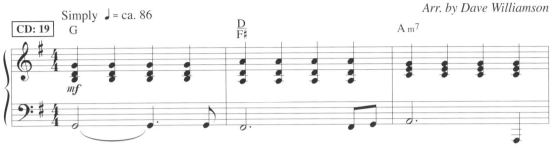

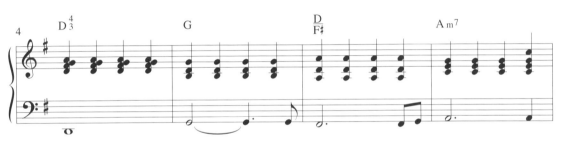

Copyright © 2008 by Pilot Point Music (ASCAP). All rights reserved.
Administered by The Copyright Company, PO Box 128139, Nashville, TN 37212-8139.

PLEASE NOTE: Copying of this product is NOT covered by CCLI licenses. For CCLI information call 1-800-234-2446.

Most High

Underscore

DAVE WILLIAMSON
Arr. by Dave Williamson

NARRATOR *(without music)*: Jesus certainly fulfilled every promise of a deliverer. He healed the sick, He could feed an army with bread from heaven, He even raised the dead! Once they even tried to crown Him King.

(Music begins) But from the beginning they were a divided people. Some received Him gladly. Others had questions. He was just not what they expected. He was too familiar, too common and humble to be a King. Some rejected Him outright "Why does your Master eat with tax collectors and other sinners?" they asked His disciples.

Others said, "If the Messiah does come, will he do more miracles than this Man? Many were experiencing what the prophet Isaiah had said about the Messiah, "He had no form that we should look at Him, no beauty that we should desire Him."

His disciples did not want Him to go to Jerusalem that final week. *(Son of the Most High begins)* And when He did, they certainly did not expect Him to give up without a fight. Especially after His entry into the city, riding in as a King in triumph, all the people shouting, "Hosanna!"

When they saw him submit to betrayal, trial, and torture, they went from belief to a state of disbelief. They just didn't understand.

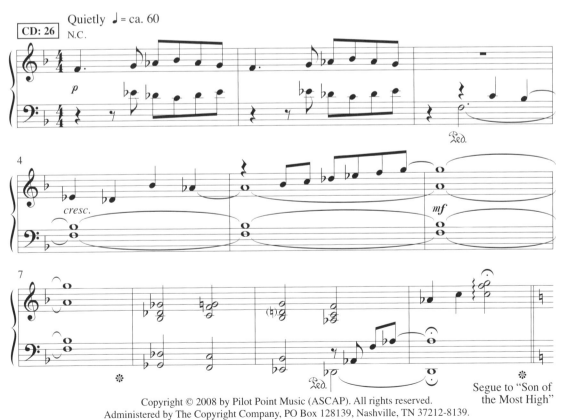

Segue to "Son of the Most High"

Copyright © 2008 by Pilot Point Music (ASCAP). All rights reserved.
Administered by The Copyright Company, PO Box 128139, Nashville, TN 37212-8139.

PLEASE NOTE: Copying of this product is NOT covered by CCLI licenses. For CCLI information call 1-800-234-2446.

Son of the Most High

Words and Music by
PHIL MEHRENS
Arr. by Dave Williamson

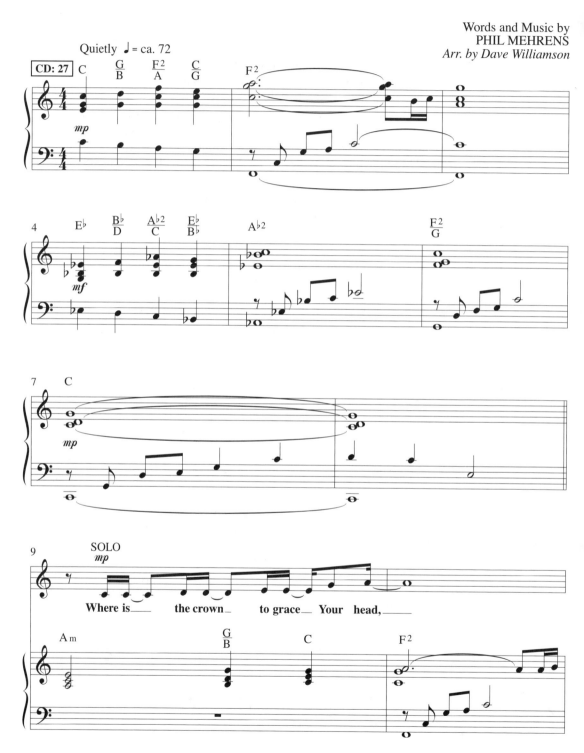

Copyright © 2008 by Pilot Point Music (ASCAP). All rights reserved.
Administered by The Copyright Company, PO Box 128139, Nashville, TN 37212-8139.

PLEASE NOTE: Copying of this product is NOT covered by CCLI licenses. For CCLI information call 1-800-234-2446.

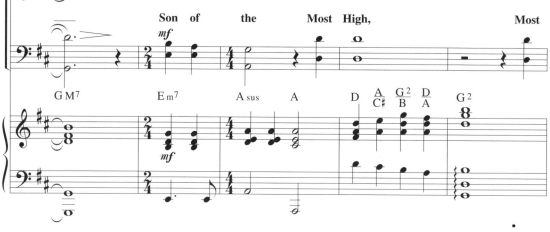
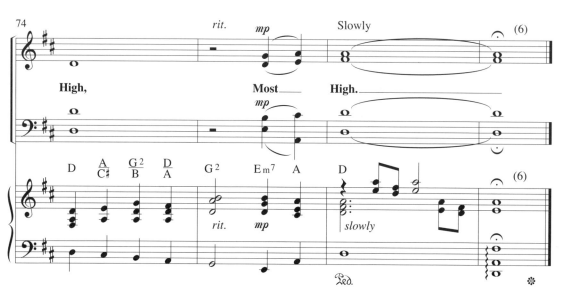

NARRATOR *(without music)*: They did not understand that is was necessary for the Christ, the King to suffer for the sin of the world and then enter into His glory. All they could do was trust in what He said and follow Him, even though it might mean following Him to death.

They didn't know that by watching Him in the final hours of His life, they would become His witnesses to testify to the world about the greatest event in history. This event would also dramatically change them. *(Music begins)* They would learn to follow their Lord even when they were uncertain where the road would lead, even when they did not understand His plan. They would learn what it means to call Him "Lord."

NARRATOR *(without music)*: There were so many presumptions about the coming King. But they came by them honestly. Many of the prophecies predicting the Messiah combine His first and second comings. After all, this mystery was hidden by God to be revealed at the proper time.

Jesus came the first time to deal with sin as a suffering Servant but in His second coming, He is the exalted Christ who comes in great glory and power to reign as King of kings and Lord of lords.

(Music begins) There is no way to express what it felt like for the disciples to go from their worst fears to the heights of joy. But that is what happened on the greatest day of all time.

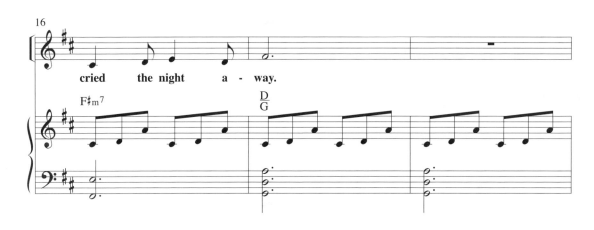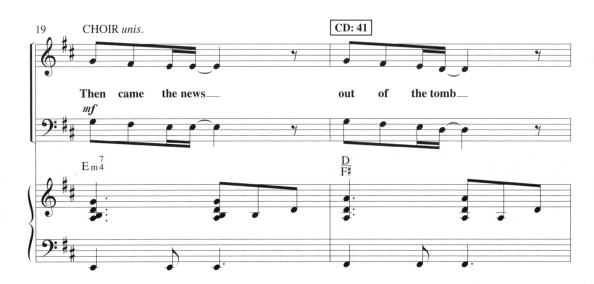

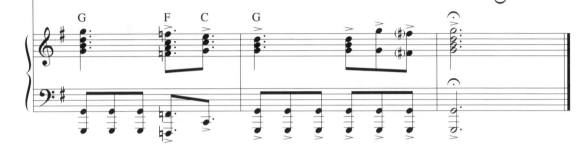

NARRATOR *(without music)*: At His trial the leaders of Israel asked Jesus directly, "Are you the Son of God?" He said "I Am . . . and you will see the Son of Man *(music begins)* sitting at the right hand of the Mighty One and coming on the clouds of Heaven." *(Mark 14:62)*

After His resurrection Jesus said, "All authority has been given to me in Heaven and on earth"

Enthroned

Words and Music by
PHIL MEHRENS and
MARTY FUNDERBURK
Arr. by Dave Williamson

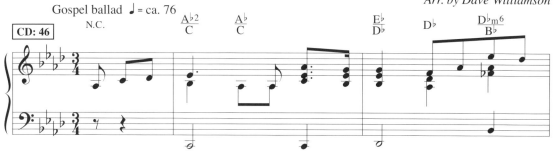
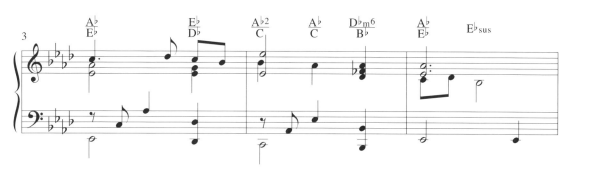
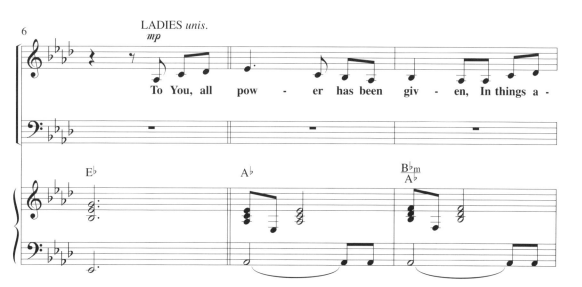

© 2008 Pilot Point Music (ASCAP) (Administered by The Copyright Company,
PO Box 128139, Nashville, TN 37212-8139)/Winding Way Music (ASCAP)
(a div. of Daywind Music Group). All rights reserved.

PLEASE NOTE: Copying of this product is NOT covered by CCLI licenses. For CCLI information call 1-800-234-2446.

Enthroned
Underscore

PHIL MEHRENS and
MARTY FUNDERBURK
Arr. by Dave Williamson

NARRATOR *(without music)*: . . . I looked, and behold, in the midst of the throne and of the four living creatures, and in the midst of the elders, stood a Lamb as though it had been slain . . . and the twenty-four elders fell down fell down before the Lamb . . . And they sang a new song, saying: "You are worthy . . . for You were slain. *(Music begins)* You have redeemed us to God by Your blood out of every tribe and tongue and people and nation, and have made us kings and priests to our God; and we shall reign on the earth."

Then I looked, and I heard the voice of many angels around the throne, the living creatures, and the elders; and the number of them was ten thousand times ten thousand . . . saying with a loud voice:

CHOIR and NARRATOR: "Worthy is the Lamb who was slain to receive power and riches and wisdom, and strength and honor and glory and blessing!" *(Revelation Song begins)*

NARRATOR: And every creature which is in heaven and on the earth and under the earth and in the sea, . . . I heard saying:

CHOIR and NARRATOR: "Blessing and honor and glory and power be to Him who sits on the throne, and to the Lamb, forever and ever!" *(Rev 5:6-13)*

© 2008 Pilot Point Music (ASCAP) (Administered by The Copyright Company,
PO Box 128139, Nashville, TN 37212-8139)/Winding Way Music (ASCAP)
(a div. of Daywind Music Group). All rights reserved.

PLEASE NOTE: Copying of this product is NOT covered by CCLI licenses. For CCLI information call 1-800-234-2446.

Revelation Song

Words and Music by
JENNIE LEE RIDDLE
Arr. by Dave Williamson

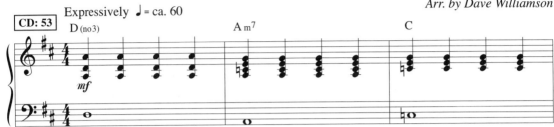
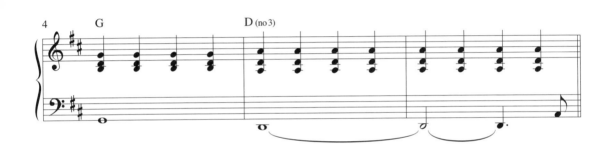

© 2004 Gateway Create Publishing/BMI (admin. by Integrity's Praise! Music)
c/o Integrity Media, Inc., 1000 Cody Road, Mobile, AL 36695.
All rights reserved. International copyright secured. Used by permission.

PLEASE NOTE: Copying of this product is NOT covered by CCLI licenses. For CCLI information call 1-800-234-2446.

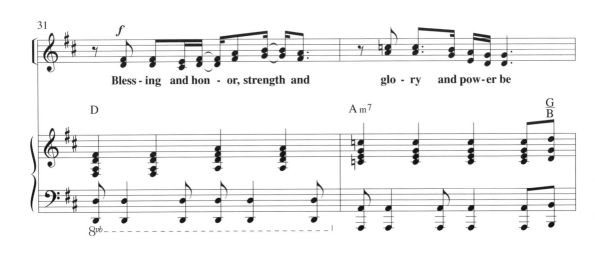

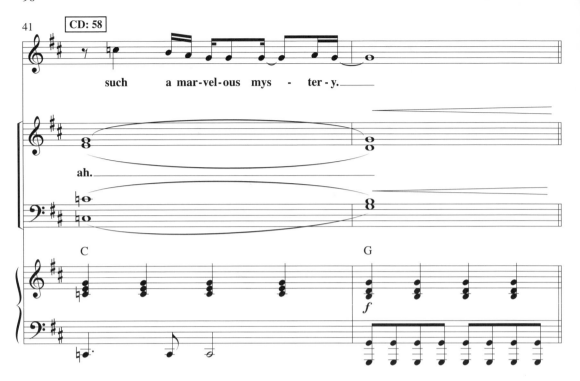
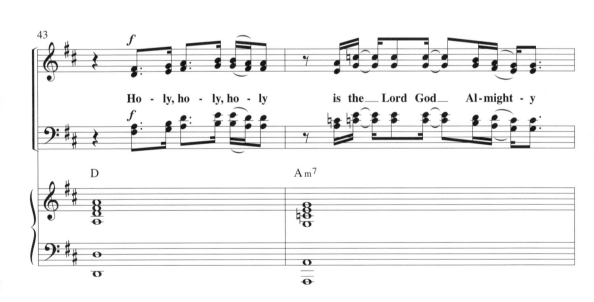

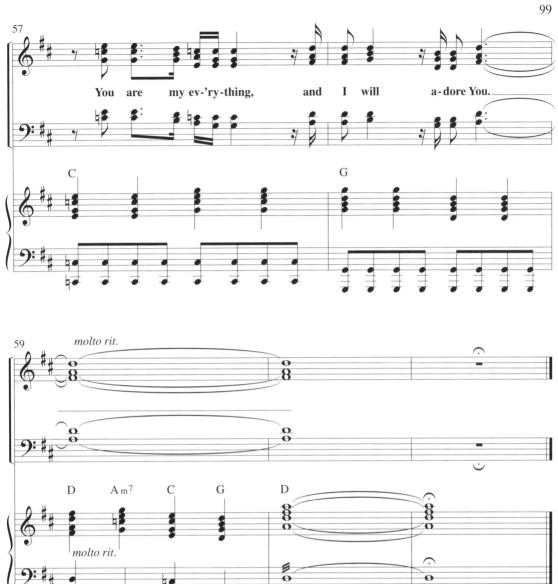

Sovereign Lord Finale

includes
Praise to the Lord, the Almighty
He Will Rule the World

Arr. by Dave Williamson

*Words by JOACHIM NEANDER and PHIL MEHRENS; Music by *Stralsund Gesangbuch* and PHIL MEHRENS.

Copyright © 2008 by Pilot Point Music (ASCAP). All rights reserved.
Administered by The Copyright Company, PO Box 128139, Nashville, TN 37212-8139.

PLEASE NOTE: Copying of this product is NOT covered by CCLI licenses. For CCLI information call 1-800-234-2446.